D0464325

A Passion for Chocolate

How to turn your love affair with chocolate into a deep and lasting relationship.

PAMELA ALLARDICE ~ *recipes by* AARON MAREE

Angus&Robertson
An imprint of HarperCollins*Publishers*

CONT

ENTS

Introduction

The love of chocolate has a long and interesting history. In addition to its use as a flavouring or candy (sweetmeat), its popular use as a drink stretches far back in time. The story of cocoa as a drink began in tropical South America. For hundreds of years the cocoa tree, *Theobroma cacao*, grew wild there. It was then cultivated, first by the Mayan Indians from the early seventh century, and then the Incas of Peru and the Aztecs of Mexico in the forests of Central and South America. 'Chocolate', in fact, is thought to be a corruption of the Nahuatl word *cacauatl,* a combination of the Aztec words for chocolate and for water, and refers solely to the drink made from the beans of the *cacao* tree. Trade flourished, so much so that the cocoa bean became a unit of currency between tribes in the area. Purchase prices are fascinating: a pumpkin, for instance, cost about four cocoa nibs, while a 'tolerably good' slave could cost up to one hundred. Sex, passion and chocolate seem to have all gone together in these early times, too, with prostitutes asking an average price of ten cocoa nibs for their favours. The Mayan Indians were well aware of the cocoa bean's properties — they used a drink made from it to appease their gods. They also boiled their cocoa beans with maize. Cocoa beans were also commonly traded, being widely prized as the source of a most pleasurable drink. In ancient Mexico, chocolate became a popular national drink, and was drunk and the beans offered in many ceremonious rituals.

A Passion FOR CHOCOLATE

Chocolate was served to brave warriors but withheld from cowards. There was a curse for any such weakling: 'He will not receive tobacco. He will not drink chocolate. He will not eat fine foods'.

The planting of the cocoa beans was a special ritual in itself. Historians record that 'tillers of the soil must sleep apart from their wives and concubines for several days in order that on the night before planting they might indulge their passions to the fullest extent'. There was even a special god whose task it was to oversee the fortunes of the cocoa planters — Ekchuah. A festival was held in Ekchuah's honour which seems to be less bloodthirsty than most of the other rituals favoured by the Mayan Indians. At least Ekchuah only demanded the sacrifice of a dog with a cocoa-coloured spot, not a human as was more often the case.

The last Aztec emperor Montezuma, it is said, preferred his chocolate flavoured with spices and then thickened with cornflour and beaten to a froth, rather like the consistency of honey. In his court, cocoa was drunk out of ornate golden goblets — at the rate of 50 large jars a day for himself and his attendants alone. Montezuma is said to have regarded this drink as an aphrodisiac and eyewitnesses at the time of the Spanish conquest noted that attendants '... brought him in cups of pure gold a drink made from the cocoa plant, which they said he took before visiting his wives.' Records go so far as to detail the very atmosphere which the mighty Emperor demanded for the occasion: 'While he was dining, the guards in the adjoining rooms did not dare speak or make a noise above a whisper ...As soon as the great Montezuma had dined, ... other

olate A Passion for chocolate A Passion
a Passion
CHOCOLATE
olate A Passion for chocolate A Passion

Indians told him jokes and others sang and danced, for Montezuma was very fond of music and entertainment and would reward his entertainers with the leavings of the food and chocolate...'

Certainly, it was not the delicious beverage we know today, because it was unsweetened and the spices used included chillies and pepper! Cinnamon was another spice much used by the early Mexicans in conjunction with cocoa and, even now, Mexican chocolate often comes ready-flavoured with cinnamon. Vanilla, yet another native spice of South America, is also a traditional companion to chocolate and is often blended into chocolate at the manufacturing stage. (It is interesting to learn that chocolate continued to be used as an ingredient in savoury dishes long after the Spanish decided it tasted nicer sweet. To this day, in Italy, you can buy chocolate pasta and tagliatelle; other traditional Mexican recipes include braised pigeon or duck with chocolate, rabbit with chocolate sauce and a remarkable turkey dish which features a chocolate and chilli sauce!)

Christopher Columbus was actually the first to come across chocolate in the New World, partaking of the drink in what is now Nicaragua in about 1502. Even though he brought samples of the beans home to Spain for presentation to King Ferdinand, neither of them seemed too impressed and chocolate's international future languished temporarily. It remained for the Emperor Montezuma to introduce his preferred recipe, *xocotlatl*, to Hernando Cortez, conqueror of Mexico, in 1519.

It is interesting to learn that, in fact, Montezuma only did so out of fear and reverence for Cortez — he thought that the Spanish soldier was the magnificent serpent god Quetzalcoatl of Aztec mythology, and so worthy of being offered chocolate. According to legend, the plumed serpent-god Quetzalcoatl bestowed the cacao tree on the early people of Mexico; Xochiquetzal, the goddess of love and happiness, adorned it with beautiful blossoms. The fruits of the cacao tree were thus much sought after by priests and nobles of Quetzalcoatl's court, being used as money and also symbols of a person's wealth. Perhaps if he had realised his error, chocolate would have remained a secret for even longer. Poor Montezuma was cruelly murdered by the conquerors, who ravaged his city and took his treasures with them.

CASANOVA considered chocolate to be a better aphrodisiac than champagne. By the 17th century, chocolate's powers as an aphrodisiac were touted by no less than Madame du Barry, who fed it to her boyfriends.

Cortez had a sweeter tooth than Montezuma and liked to take his royal drink with extra sugar. Physicians travelling with Cortez were intrigued by the drink's seeming ability to bestow fortitude and strength on those who partook of it. Cortez himself reported to the King of Spain that 'A cup of this precious drink permits a man to walk for a whole day without food.' No wonder it was heralded as one of the 'treasures' of the New World. Following his discovery of the cocoa tree

FOR

Chocolate is rich in magnesium, the essential mineral that hits a monthly low during the menstrual cycle, which may be the reason women binge on chocolate to relieve the PMS blues. Chocolate also contains phenylethylamine, a natural amino acid that elevates moods. This is one reason which scientists give in explaining chocolate's ability to give energy.

in Mexico, Hernando Cortez took beans with him and planted them in Haiti and Trinidad on his way back to Spain.

Back at the court of Spain, King Charles V became besotted with the new drink. It was thanks to him that a new, higher style of cup was developed, for the serving of chocolate. Fashionable accessories for the 16th century chocoholic included silver chocolate pots on highly decorated platters with matching cups and spoons. Special swizzle sticks, usually made from chased silver, were placed on the serving tray so the drinkers could whisk their beverage into a fresh froth, as they desired. The Spaniards experimented with the drink, substituting milk or cream for the water and sweetening it with sugar.

At first the import of cocoa beans was jealously restricted to Spain. As the Spanish empire spread, so too did the production of cocoa, with vast plantations being opened up through Venezuela, the African coast and even the Philippines around this time. Although the Spanish were unable to keep secret the method of preparation, chocolate remained an expensive luxury. Interestingly, the process of preparing the cocoa itself, from the raw beans into small dried tablets or powder, gradually fell to the monasteries, who enjoyed quite a spectacular profit from this activity until major commercial manufacturers became involved elsewhere within Europe. Convents, too, vied with each other for the honour of perfecting the best chocolate recipe.

By the 17th century, drinking chocolate had been introduced to the courts of Italy, Germany, France and England. As it continued its conquest of Europe, apart from being much enjoyed for its exotic taste, chocolate also quickly attracted a reputation as being something of a cure-all. Men and women drank it in the hope of curing all manner of ills, children were encouraged to drink it to help them sleep and study better, and matrons drank it in the hope of making themselves beautiful enough to attract young suitors!

However, not everyone had a passion for chocolate at first. It came under papal fire in 1569 when Pope Pius V, served a cup, found it so disgusting that he claimed it did *not* need to be banned at Lent, for people in their right minds would not regard it as a luxury, anyway! His words fell on unheeding ears, it seems. Another main reason for the ecclesiastical controversy surrounding chocolate was that it was thought to 'inflame the passions'. In 1624, a 'Disputation' was issued which forbade the monks who prepared chocolate to take more than a certain amount themselves, to 'avoid scandal'.

At one point the Bishop of Chiapa attempted to put a stop to the 'sacrilegious' craze of women who 'pretending such weakness and squeamishness of the stomach ... bring (with) them to church in the middle of Mass or sermon a cup of chocolate.' The women reproached him and there was quite an uproar amongst the congregation who protested about the withdrawal of their 'medicine'. Perhaps there are sinister overtones in the fact that the Bishop of Chiapa died shortly afterwards, apparently from a poisoned drink ... (Nor was this the sole case of death by chocolate.

Rumour has it that Charles II, who died in 1685, was given a cup of poisoned chocolate by his spurned mistress, the Duchess of Portsmouth.)

France took chocolate to its heart with the arrival of the Spanish princess, Anne of Austria, who arrived in 1655 to marry the then infant king, Louis XIII. She brought with her many fine jewels and gowns, along with a supply of cocoa beans to prepare her favourite breakfast drink. One of her dowry gifts was a beautifully carved and gilded 'chocolate box', filled with the little dried chocolate cakes which were at that time used in the preparation of drinking chocolate. She even brought with her a special maid, known as 'La Molina', whose sole task was to make her mistress's chocolate. The Queen's invitations 'to drink chocolate' rapidly became prized as a high point in the social calendar of the court.

Soon merchants of other nationalities were buying the beans and growing them where the climate was suitable. Adventurer and speculator Giramolo Benzoni, who set out from his native Milan around this time to go to the New World, recorded his first experience with chocolate given him by the local Indians: '... subsequently, wine failing, and unwilling to drink nothing but water, I did as others did. The flavour is somewhat bitter, but it satisfies and refreshes the body without intoxicating: the Indians esteem it above everything, wherever they are accustomed to it.'

However, even as it became more available throughout Europe, chocolate remained a luxury for many years, its price ensuring that it remained only

a treat for the wealthy. In fact, in most countries, cocoa became a substantial source of revenue and was highly taxed. The only country which was the exception to this rule was Austria, where it was, and probably would still be regarded as, the national drink. France followed suit towards the beginning of the 1700s, when a royal warrant was issued specifying that the price of cocoa could not exceed a fixed price — back then, it was a mere four francs a pound — and that the sale itself of chocolate should be free from tax.

The English were well aware of cocoa and drinking chocolate. An early English explorer, Thomas Gage, had reported as early as 1648 on its use in the West Indies, although he was not greatly impressed with the way it was made there, calling it a 'spicy, scummy drink'. Unsurprising, when you read of how it was made: 'The Cinnamon and the long red Pepper are to be first beaten with the Anniseed, and then the Cacao ... When it is well beaten and incorporated, the manner of drinking it, is divers; the one (being the way most us'd in Mexico) is to take it hot with *atolle* (a cornmeal gruel drink), dissolving a Tablet in

Hot Water, and then stirring and beating it in the Cup where it is to be drunk, with a *molinet* (a wooden stick carved especially for mixing chocolate), and when it is well stirr'd to a scum or froth, then to fill the cup with hot *atolle* and so drink it sup by sup.'

Although the Spanish monopoly of the chocolate trade was broken in 1606 by one Antonio Carletti, an Italian explorer who took the recipe home to Italy, it was not until the capture of Jamaica in 1655 that the English were able to get their hands on some thriving cocoa plantations, and so circumvent the trade stranglehold which the Dutch and the Spanish had created. When the first chocolate house opened in London in Bishopsgate in 1657, chocolate cost from 10 to 15 shillings a pound. The drink itself was advertised as 'an excellent West Indian beverage ... you may have made ready at any time.' Chocolate houses swiftly became important meeting places for the fashionable and wealthy in England — Swifts and White's were two very popular chocolate houses. During Queen Anne's reign, the Cocoa Tree was a 'political' house frequented by Tories.

Samuel Pepys was one of the first regular patrons of chocolate houses, and soon made it a morning habit to 'take chocolate'. He dubbed the drink 'delicious ... but rather expensive'. He also favoured chocolate as a hangover cure. He wrote of the sorry state of his head after celebrating the coronation of King Charles II in 1661: 'Waked in the morning with my head in a sad taking through last night's drink, which I am very sorry for. So rose and went with Mr Creed to drink our morning draught, which he did give me in chocolate to settle my stomach.'

The fashion soon crossed the Channel and chocolate houses appeared in Paris. One of the most famous was the Café Procope which boasted Napoleon and Verlaine amongst its patrons. Exquisite and leisured ladies, like Despina in Mozart's *Cosi fan Tutte*, retained troupes of maids to beat their chocolate for up to an hour at a time before they would deign to drink it — the poor maids, of course, could do no more than just sniff it. Queen Maria, on her marriage to Louis XIV, presented her husband with an exquisite 'chocolate casket' as a gift. Madame de Pompadour even commissioned a complete porcelain 'chocolate service' from the exquisite Sèvres factory. The unusual pot, with its characteristic right-handed handle and spout, may still be seen today.

There was even a romantic story attached to the first Viennese chocolate house. There a serving girl, named Anna Baltauf, offered chocolate to the Crown Prince Dietrich, who promptly fell in love with the drink (and, presumably, with her as well) and married her. As a wedding gift, he had her painted wearing her maid's outfit by the noted Swiss artist, Jean-Etienne Liotard. This painting, dubbed 'La Belle Chocolatier', was later to be used as the illustration in advertisements for America's Baker's Chocolate.

By the early 18th century, all of Europe was chocolate-addicted. Many experiments and innovations came in and out of fashion. Some chocolate houses added claret and egg yolks to their brew for their 'strengthening' properties. Others created a type of custard with arrowroot and milk. In 1756, Prince Wilhelm von Schaumburg-Lippe founded a chocolate factory in Steinhude in Germany, using Portuguese labour, and soon chocolate factories blossomed elsewhere throughout Europe, especially Austria and Switzerland. Hot chocolate or *chachaletto* — it had previously been served cold — became the rage in coffee houses in Europe as well as colonial America, where it outsold both coffee and tea. Chocolate production came full circle from Europe back to America in 1765, when the first chocolate processing house opened in Dorchester, Massachusetts.

Then, in 1826, came the beginning of real change in the eating of chocolate. English firm J.S. Fry and Sons advertised a chocolate lozenge or bar — 'a pleasant and nutritious substitute for food while travelling or when unusual fasting is caused by an irregular period of mealtimes.' Following hard on their heels came Coenraad Van Houten's invention of the process of 'dutching'. This was a method of removing the fat from the dried cocoa cake and therefore producing both a powder —which could then be mixed into biscuits and used as a flavouring agent — and a pure type of cocoa butter. This latter product, cocoa butter, was to form the basis of quality 'eating chocolate', as we know it today.

After 300 years of use as a drink, solid 'eating' chocolate — created by combining cocoa butter with chocolate liquor and sugar — was developed by a British firm, Fry's Chocolate, in 1847. Two years later Henri Nestlé of Switzerland created 'milk' chocolate. It is interesting to note that all the early 'great names' of chocolate making — Fry's, Cadbury's, Rowntree, Nestlé, Séchaud, Tobler, Perugina and Lindt in Europe, for instance, and Mars, See's, Boldemann's and Hershey's in America — are with us still.

The slogan for Cadbury's Cocoa — 'Makes strong men stronger' — remained in use for almost twenty years. The rest of the advertisement goes on to describe the benefits of the product in glowing, healthful terms: 'Gives strength and staying power to athletes. Exhilarating, comforting and sustaining ... providing, in concentrated form, admirable nutritive flesh-forming qualities, strength, and staying power.' Their arch rival, Fry's, prepared a special campaign during World War I featuring wounded soldiers sipping on chocolate while recuperating, above the slogan: 'For convalescents and others, there is no better food.' Before the advent of more rigid controls over what could and could not be claimed in advertising, Cadbury took aim at its competitors with a new ditty:

'To adulterate cocoa's become such a practise
That really the State must step in to protect us,
The faculty tells us to drink, but the fact is

The stuff is so starched they can hardly expect us
Who wish for pure cocoa in all its quintessence
Will certainly find it in Cadbury's Essence.'

'Chocolate is not only pleasant to taste,
but it is also a veritable balm of the mouth,
for the maintaining of all glands and humours
in a good state of health. Thus it is, that all
who drink it, possess a sweet breath.'

Doctor Stephani Blancardi,
Amsterdam, 1705

America is surely the most avid chocolate-loving nation on earth. They even sport an astonishing 'chocolate theme park' and a town named Hersheyville in Pennsylvania, home of the Hershey Bar! The Hershey empire was started by Milton Snaveley Hershey in the early 20th century. He was so impressed with the potential of the German-made chocolate-making machinery which was on display at the Chicago Exposition of 1893 that he bought the exhibit, lock, stock and barrel, and set up business immediately. Hershey's biggest contribution to world chocolate consumption came during the Second World War, when the American government asked them to develop an 'energy bar' which could survive tropical climates in a soldier's pocket. American consumption of luxury chocolates is twice what it was a decade ago, although it still lags behind Austria, Belgium, Norway and Germany. Exports of Swiss chocolate, however, have risen four times as fast as worldwide annual chocolate sales since 1988.

The Cocoa Tree

All chocolate products are based upon cocoa in varying amounts. The cocoa tree is a native of the equatorial forests and flourishes in rich, deep, loose soils. Today, the best cocoa plantations are to be found in West Africa, around the

Ivory Coast, Nigeria and the Cameroon. These areas are the largest exporters, followed by Brazil and Ecuador. For healthy growth, cocoa trees prefer an average shade temperature of around 27°C and an annual rainfall of at least 1900 mm. The tree is rather like an apple tree in size and shape, growing about seven metres high. They take about five to eight years from planting to return their first harvest and, when mature, yield two harvests a year. One of the oldest engravings in existence, depicting a Mayan Indian farmer, shows a 'mother tree' — or protective shade tree — being planted to shade a delicate young cocoa tree, and this is still common practice on even very large plantations.

The fruit itself looks rather like a small football. As it ripens it changes colour, from green through yellow and orange to purple when fully ripe. Each cacao bean is quite nutritionally rich, being comprised of 40 per cent carbohydrates, 23 per cent fat and 18 per cent protein, with traces of riboflavin, calcium, and iron. The beans and pulp are allowed to ferment together when they are harvested, and it is this which gives the beans their characteristic and somewhat bitter flavour.

The beans are then dried in the sun and the shells of the beans removed, leaving the kernel, or 'nib'. These nibs are ground to a thick dark paste the consistency of liquid cream, called chocolate liquor. This is then pressed between heavy heated rollers which remove the fat or cocoa butter and leave a dry powdery mass which is ground into cocoa powder and shipped to other countries for production. Manufacturing methods have been much improved in the last century, in order to meet increased demand for chocolate products.

TYPES OF CHOCOLATE

Cocoa

Cocoa is a powdered, pure chocolate product that has a slightly bitter flavour as it contains no added sugar. Cocoa is a convenient way to achieve a strong chocolate flavour, particularly in baked goods where no other fat or liquid is required. For best results, cocoa should be sifted with other dry ingredients or blended to a paste with hot liquid. Cocoa is very good to use in pastries, biscuits and cakes.

Drinking chocolate

This is cocoa combined with sugar. It dissolves easily, and its prime use is in drinks. It may be used in place of cocoa in cookery should a milder flavour be desirable. Drinking chocolate is ideal for coatings and icings and also gives an excellent finish when dusted or sprinkled over food, such as cakes or truffles.

Malted chocolate

A combination of cocoa, malt grains and sugar. Again, this is primarily intended for drinks, but can be used in baking cakes to give a light and distinctive flavour.

Confectioner's chocolate

Also known as *couverture*, this is the richly flavoured chocolate which is primarily used in professional baking and confectionery production. It contains a higher than usual proportion of cocoa butter, which gives it a glossy appearance and a smooth texture. It is more expensive than other kinds of chocolate.

Bittersweet chocolate

This is the term used to describe plain, unsweetened or dark chocolate which contains a minimum of 34 per cent cocoa solids. The best results in cooking are obtained by using a deluxe bittersweet chocolate which contains up to 50 per cent solids. Interestingly, this type of chocolate usually contains more sugar than milk chocolate, in order to counteract the natural bitterness. It is darker and slightly more bitter than regular dark chocolate, and is made from a highly roasted cocoa bean rather than just a sun-dried one. Many chocolate *aficionados* tend to prefer the less sweet flavour.

Milk chocolate

This was originally made in the mid-19th century, and credit is usually given to Henri Nestlé for the invention, although some sources say it was a Dr Hans Sloane, an 18th century physician, who was first to create it.

It is thought that Nestlé's version of milk chocolate was made with condensed milk (he was working on a baby food formula at the time!) but it is now made using dried and powdered milk. Milk chocolate does not contain as much chocolate liquor as regular chocolate which results in a milder, smoother flavour. It is less suitable for cooking than regular chocolate.

White chocolate

White chocolate is not really chocolate at all. It is a blend of cocoa butter and milk solids, but it does not contain any chocolate liquor, hence its colour. Though it is the least stable to work with, it is popular for its distinctive flavour, creamy texture and its colour contrast to other chocolates. White chocolate is particularly popular for use with summer fruits. For best results, compound white cooking chocolate should be used in cold desserts such as mousses and puddings.

Blocks

Blocks of cooking chocolate are very convenient for decorative uses, such as neat chocolate shavings or chocolate curls. They can easily be broken into even pieces for weighing and melting prior to cooking.

a Passion FOR CHOCOLATE

Heaven Sent

Although these cakes are absolute heaven to both view and taste, you must be aware that they can be devilish on the hips. Each is perfect for any lover of chocolate — whenever the craving strikes!

Chocolate Cream Puffs

A DESSERT-TO-DIE-FOR

1 cup (250 ml/8 fl oz) water
90 g (3 oz) unsalted butter
¼ cup (100 g/3½ oz) plain flour, sifted
1½ tablespoons (15 g/½ oz) cocoa, sifted
4 to 5 x 60 g (2 oz) eggs
icing sugar or cocoa for dusting
1 quantity Creamy Chocolate Mousse *(see page 28)*

1 Preheat the oven to 200°C (400°F).

2 Place the water and butter in a saucepan and bring slowly to the boil. While the mixture is boiling, stir in the flour and cocoa. Continue stirring vigorously as the mixture cooks and until it leaves the sides of the pan and forms a solid ball (approx. 2 minutes).

3 Beat in four eggs one at a time until the mixture becomes smooth and shiny. Remove from heat. (If the mixture requires, add the last egg.) Stop beating. The mixture is ready when a knife run through it leaves behind a trail.

4 Place large tablespoons of the batter onto a lightly greased tray and bake in the oven for 35 to 40 minutes. To prevent steam from escaping, do not open the oven door for the first 15 minutes.

5 When baked, pierce a small hole in the base of each puff to allow internal steam to escape. Allow puffs to cool. Scoop out any uncooked mixture.

6 When cold cut in half and fill with *Creamy Chocolate Mousse*.

7 Dust the top with icing sugar.

MAKES 12

Featherlight Gâteau

A GORGEOUS NAME FOR A SINFULLY GORGEOUS GATEAU.

125 g (4 oz) unsalted butter
250 g (8 oz) dark cooking chocolate, chopped
6 x 60 g (2 oz) eggs, separated
⅓ cup (75 g/2½ oz) caster sugar
1½ tablespoons plain flour
24 chocolate squares, or 24 after dinner mints
cocoa, for dusting

1 Preheat the oven to 180°C (350°F).

2 Grease and lightly flour a 24 cm (9½ in) round springform cake pan.

3 Melt the butter and chopped chocolate in the top of a double boiler, stirring to combine.

4 Beat the egg yolks and sugar until thick and pale. Fold the melted chocolate mixture into the egg yolk mixture and mix until well combined. Gently fold in the flour.

5 Beat the egg whites until stiff peaks form and then gently fold through the egg yolk mixture.

6 Pour three-quarters of the mixture into the prepared pan and bake for 40 minutes.

7 When baked the cake should have shrunk slightly from the sides of the pan. Allow it to cool in the pan and it should sink in the middle as it cools.

8 When completely cool, remove the sides of the pan from the cake and pour the reserved quarter of the mixture into the hollow on top of the cake. Take a little of the mixture and spread it thickly around the sides of the cake, spreading the remainder evenly over the top.

9 Place the cake onto a plate or serving dish and then begin arranging the chocolate squares around the sides, making certain that each one overlaps the others. Cut remaining squares into triangles with a hot knife and then press these triangles into the top of the cake.

10 Refrigerate cake for 1 hour, then remove and dust with cocoa powder before cutting with a hot knife to serve.

SERVES 12

Creamy Chocolate Mousse

120 g (4 oz) cream cheese
$\frac{2}{3}$ cup (150 g/5 oz) caster sugar
2 x 60 g (2 oz) egg yolks
$2\frac{1}{2}$ cups (600 ml/20 fl oz) thickened cream
125 g (4 oz) dark cooking chocolate, melted
125 g (4 oz) milk cooking chocolate, melted

sion

ATE

1 Beat cream cheese, sugar and egg yolks until smooth.

2 Whip cream until stiff and return to refrigerator.

3 Quickly stir melted chocolate into cream cheese mixture and fold through whipped cream by hand.

4 Fill *Chocolate Cream Puffs*.

MAKES SUFFICIENT FILLING FOR 12 PUFFS.

Triple Chocolate Surprise

IMPOSSIBLE TO RESIST, THIS SUMPTUOUS CAKE FEATURES THREE TYPES OF CHOCOLATE.

100 g (3½ oz) unsalted butter, softened
⅔ cup (100 g/3½ oz) brown sugar
1 x 60 g (2 oz) egg
60 g (2 oz) dark cooking chocolate, melted
90 g (3 oz) sour cream
2 tablespoons (40 ml/1½ fl oz) milk
1 cup (135 g/4½ oz) plain flour, sifted
1 teaspoon bicarbonate soda
3 tablespoons cocoa

WHITE CHOCOLATE CREAM

⅔ cup (160 ml/4½ fl oz) thickened cream
2 tablespoons (30 g/1 oz) icing sugar, sifted
60 g (2 oz) unsalted butter
200 g (7 oz) white cooking chocolate, chopped

MILK CHOCOLATE CREAM

⅓ cup (80 ml/2½ fl oz) thickened cream
2 tablespoons (30 g/1 oz) icing sugar, sifted
60 g (2 oz) unsalted butter
200 g (7 oz) milk cooking chocolate, chopped

Dark Chocolate Cream

½ cup (125 ml/4 fl oz) thickened cream
250 g (8 oz) dark cooking chocolate, chopped

Chocolate Curls

150 g (5 oz) white chocolate buttons
150 g (5 oz) milk chocolate buttons
150 g (5 oz) dark chocolate buttons

1 Preheat the oven to 180°C (350°F).

2 Lightly grease a 19 x 19 x 7 cm (7¼ x 7¼ x 2½ in) square cake pan and line with baking paper.

3 Cream butter and sugar together until light and fluffy. Add the egg and combine well. (Mixture may curdle slightly, but do not worry). Add the melted chocolate to the butter mixture and beat in quickly before the chocolate sets.

4 Mix the sour cream and the milk together and add to the chocolate butter mixture along with the sifted flour, bicarbonate soda and cocoa.

5 Pour the cake mixture into the prepared pan and bake for 30 to 35 minutes.

6 Allow cake to rest in the pan for 20 minutes, then turn out onto a cake wire to cool.

7 *To Make White and Milk Chocolate Creams.* Place the cream into a saucepan with the icing sugar and butter and stir slowly while bringing to the boil. Remove the boiling liquid from the heat and immediately add the chopped chocolate. Stir until the chocolate has melted and a smooth liquid is formed. Place the liquid into a bowl and refrigerate until cold.

8. *To Make Dark Chocolate Cream*. Place cream in saucepan and stir slowly while bringing to the boil. Remove from heat, stir in chopped chocolate until melted and a smooth liquid is formed. Place liquid in a bowl and refrigerate until cold.

9 When cold, whip each of the chocolate creams separately until light and fluffy and of a spreadable consistency.

10 Cut the cake into three layers horizontally. Spread White Chocolate Cream evenly over bottom layer. Place the next layer of cake on top and spread evenly with the Milk Chocolate Cream, then place the final layer of cake on top of these and press the whole cake down firmly to ensure it is flat.

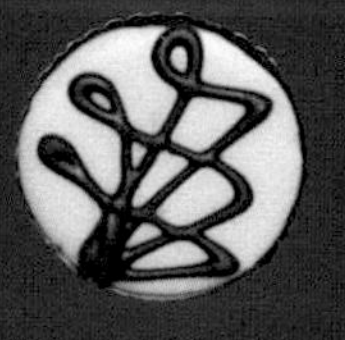

11 Spread the top and sides of the cake with the Dark Chocolate Cream. Refrigerate the cake until chocolate curls have been made.

12 *To Make Curls*. Pour melted chocolate onto a marble slab or a stainless steel countertop and use a palette knife to spread thinly. As the chocolate begins to set, hold a large knife at a 45 degree angle to the bench top and pull gently through the chocolate. It is essential to work quickly or the chocolate will harden and splinter. Curls should be 4 to 5 cm (1½ to 2 in) in length.

13 Starting in one corner of the cake, press a row of white chocolate curls over a 4 cm wide strip of the cake. Beside that place a strip of milk chocolate curls and then a strip of dark chocolate curls. Repeat in this sequence until the whole cake has been covered. Refrigerate the cake for 30 minutes before serving.

SERVES 12

a Passion
CHOCOLATE

Raspberry Fantasy

LIFE IS A DREAM WITH THIS ROMANTIC FRUITY DESSERT.

CRUST

¾ cup (100 g/3½ oz) plain flour
100 g (3½ oz) unsalted butter, softened
1 teaspoon cinnamon
40 g (1½ oz) finely chopped almonds
¼ cup (40 g/1½ oz) brown sugar

FILLING

150 g (5 oz) unsalted butter, softened
⅔ cup (150 g/5 oz) caster sugar
2 x 60 g (2 oz) eggs
100 g (3½ oz) white cooking chocolate, melted
200 g (6½ oz) fresh raspberries

TO DECORATE

fresh raspberries
chocolate curls

A PASSION FOR CHOCOLATE

1 *To Make Crust.* Gently combine the flour, butter and cinnamon. Add the almonds and brown sugar and mix until a soft paste is formed.

2 Press the mixture into a lightly greased 23 cm (9 in) round springform cake pan and bake at 180°C (350°F) for 10 minutes or until light golden brown. Allow to cool in the pan.

3 *To Make Filling.* Cream butter and sugar together until light and fluffy. Add the eggs one at a time and when combined, fold mixture through the melted chocolate.

4 Fold through the fresh raspberries and pour the mixture directly on top of the cooled base. Refrigerate for 1 hour.

5 Decorate with extra fresh raspberries and chocolate curls and serve immediately.

SERVES 12

MANY COUNTRIES BOAST A 'CLASSIC' CHOCOLATE DISH. THINK OF SACHER TORTE OR BLACK FOREST

Slice of Heaven

A DELECTABLE TREAT

FOR INCURABLE CHOCOHOLICS.

BASE

250 g (8 oz) unsalted butter, melted
150 g (5 oz) dark cooking chocolate, melted
4 x 60 g (2 oz) eggs
2½ cups (500 g/16 oz) caster sugar
1¼ cups (150 g/5 oz) plain flour

TOPPING

250 g (8 oz) unsalted butter
2 cups (360 g/12 oz) icing sugar
100 g (3½ oz) dark cooking chocolate, melted
100 g (3½ oz) marshmallows, chopped
100 g (3½ oz) chocolate dots or drops
100 g (3½ oz) macadamia nuts

DEVIL'S FOOD CAKE AND BROWNIES MEAN THE UNITED STATES, CHOCOLATE *CASSATA* AND

SION
ATE

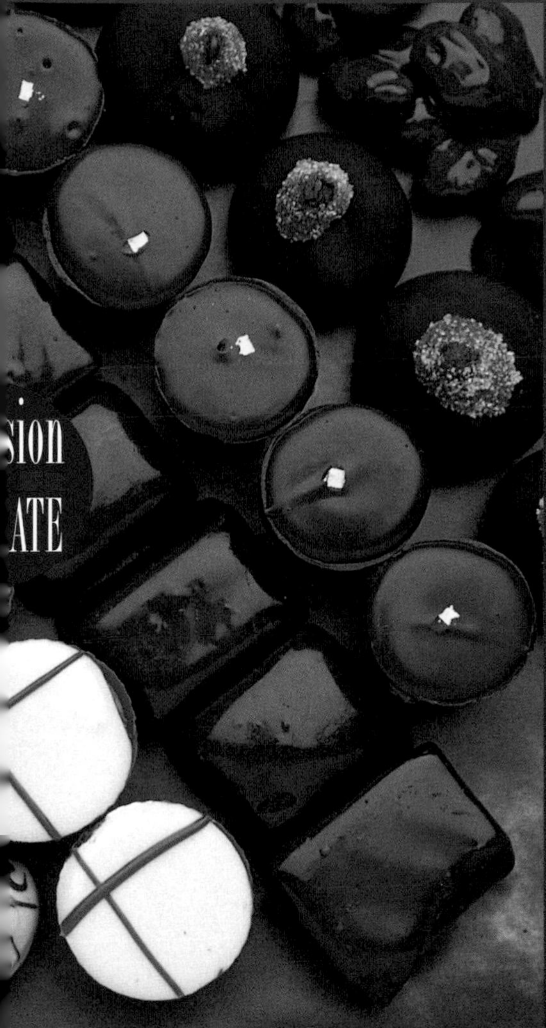

1 Preheat the oven to 160°C (325°F).

2 Grease a 25 x 30 x 3 cm (10 x 12 x 1 in) baking pan, and line with baking paper.

3 *To Make Base.* Mix the melted butter with the chocolate and whisk in the eggs until smooth. Add the sugar and flour and stir again till smooth. Spread the mixture into the prepared pan. Bake for 45 minutes or until cooked.

4 *To Make Topping.* While the base is baking, mix the butter and icing sugar together until light and fluffy. Add the melted chocolate to the butter mix and then fold through the chopped marshmallows, chocolate dots and nuts.

5 Once baked, allow the slice to cool slightly; however, while still warm, spread the topping evenly over the base. Refrigerate for 24 hours. Cut slice into portions using a hot knife.

MAKES 30 PIECES (APPROXIMATELY)

Chocolate Tart

A SIMPLY SCRUMPTIOUS TREAT, FILLED WITH RICH CHOCOLATE AND TOPPED WITH A CREAMY CHOCOLATE SAUCE.

Pastry

180 g (6 oz) unsalted butter
½ cup (90 g/3 oz) icing sugar
2 cups (240 g/8 oz) plain flour
4½ tablespoons cocoa
1 x 60 g (2 oz) egg

Filling

100 g (3½ oz) butter
100 g (3½ oz) dark cooking chocolate
3 x 60 g (2 oz) eggs
⅓ cup (45 g/1½ oz) plain flour
⅔ cup (150 g/5 oz) caster sugar

Topping

⅓ cup (90 ml/3 fl oz) thickened cream
250 g (8 oz) dark cooking chocolate, chopped

1 Preheat the oven to 150°C (300°F).

2 Lightly grease a 24 x 4 cm (9½ x 1½ in) round quiche or cake pan.

3 *To Make Pastry.* Rub the butter into the sifted dry ingredients until the mixture resembles fine breadcrumbs. Add the egg and work the mixture to a dough.

4 On a lightly floured bench, roll the dough thinly and large enough in size to fill the greased tin. Line the pan carefully with the pastry and place in the refrigerator until filling is ready.

5 *To Make Filling.* Melt the butter and chocolate together in the top of a double boiler.

6 Whisk the eggs, flour and sugar on high speed for 5 minutes. Pour the melted chocolate and butter mixture into the whisked egg mixture and stir together.

7 Pour the chocolate mixture into the pastry lined pan and bake for 35 to 45 minutes.

8 *To Make Topping.* While the tart is baking, place the cream in a saucepan and slowly bring to the boil. Remove from the heat and add the chopped chocolate, stirring until all the chocolate has dissolved. Leave the mixture in the saucepan, covered, until the tart has baked and cooled.

9 When the tart is baked, allow to cool in the pan. As it cools the crust will sink — help it to flatten by pressing it down gently.

10 When the tart is cold and the crust flattened, pour the chocolate topping over the top of it. Refrigerate for 1 hour before serving.

SERVES 8 TO 10

a Passion for CHOCOLATE

Decadent Delights

These are absolutely the ultimate desserts and treats for chocolate lovers. Only small portions should be served or total addiction will set in ...

A Bag of Fruit

HERE RICH CHOCOLATE AND LUSCIOUS FRUITS

COMBINE IN BLISSFUL HARMONY.

150 g (5 oz) dark chocolate buttons or drops, melted
A selection of fresh fruits, sliced or chopped

1 Carefully and neatly wrap a small packet or box approximately 10 x 6 x 3 cm (4 x 2½ x 1 in) with foil. Cover all but one end of the box.

2 Carefully paint all five sides with chocolate, ensuring corners are well coated. Refrigerate and repeat painting process twice.

3 When finally set, carefully slide box from chocolate and foil and remove the foil from the chocolate with tweezers. Lay the finished bag on its side on a plate and fill with an array of fresh fruits.

MAKES 1

'If any man has drunk a little too deeply from the cup of physical pleasure ;
if he has spent too much time at his desk that should have been spent asleep ;
if his fine spirits have temporarily become dulled ;
if he finds the air too damp, the minutes too slow,
and the atmosphere too heavy to withstand ;
if he is obsessed by a fixed idea which bars him from any freedom of thought :
if he is any of these poor creatures, we say,
let him be given a good pint of amber-flavoured chocolate,
in the proportions of sixty to seventy-two grains of amber to a pound,
and marvels will be performed.'

BRILLAT-SAVARIN, 'PHYSIOLOGIE DU GOUT', 1825

White Chocolate Rose Petal Mousse

A DREAMY DESSERT FOR TRUE ROMANTICS.

2 teaspoons gelatine
1½ tablespoons water
1½ tablespoons liquid glucose
2 x 60 g (2 oz) egg yolks
250 g (8 oz) white cooking chocolate, melted
2½ cups (625 ml/21 fl oz) cream, very lightly whipped
rind (zest) and juice of 1 lemon
petals of 3 medium roses, different colours, washed

RASPBERRY SAUCE

200 g (6½ oz) fresh raspberries
sugar to sweeten
2½ tablespoons cold water

1 Soak the gelatine in the water. Gently heat glucose and gelatine until melted. Add egg yolks and stir in melted chocolate. Add warm mixture immediately to cream, then add lemon juice and zest and rose petals.

2 Pour the mixture into a baking pan 25 x 30 x 3 cm (10 x 12 x 1 in) lined with cling film and refrigerate.

3 Cut the firm mousse into 5 cm (2 in) squares and serve 2 squares per serve on raspberry sauce.

4 *To Make Raspberry Sauce.* Place hulled and washed raspberries and water into a blender with enough sugar to sweeten. Purée until smooth.

MAKES 8 TO 10 PORTIONS

Chocolate Pearls on a Curacao Sauce

STYLE AND ELEGANCE FOR CHOCOHOLICS

WITH FLAIR AND TASTE.

3 x 60 g (2 oz) egg whites
½ cup (100 g/3½ oz) icing sugar, sifted
¼ cup (30 g/1 oz) plain flour, sifted
1½ teaspoons cocoa
40 g (1½ oz) unsalted butter, melted
Creamy Chocolate Mousse *(see page 28) for 6 portions*
110 g (3½ oz) dark cooking chocolate, melted
1¼ cups (300 ml/10 fl oz) Blue Curacao Liqueur
1 tablespoon arrowroot
6 white chocolate buttons

1 Preheat the oven to 180°C (350°F).

2 Mix the egg whites with the icing sugar until well blended. Add the flour and cocoa and lightly whisk until a smooth paste is formed. Allow batter to rest for 15 minutes. Stir in the melted butter and mix in well.

3 Place tablespoon amounts of the batter onto a lightly greased baking tray and spread each into a 5 to 8 cm (2 to 3 in) circle.

4 Bake for 5 to 8 minutes, then immediately remove the tuilles (biscuits) from the tray by sliding a sharp flat knife or spatula underneath each one. Each biscuit must be immediately pressed into a round container so that they will harden into semicircular shapes.

5 When the biscuits are cold and hard, lightly brush the insides of each with melted chocolate and allow to set.

6 Fill half of the tuille shells with the chocolate mousse.

7 Pipe a little melted chocolate onto a dessert plate and set the mousse-filled shell on top and hold until it sits firm. Place an unfilled shell slightly behind the filled shell so that it looks like a slightly open lid. (A little melted chocolate may be required to hold this in place). Place a white button on top of the mousse to resemble a pearl.

8 Place half the curacao into a saucepan and bring slowly to the boil. Mix the other half of the liqueur with the arrowroot and stir into the boiling liquid. Continue to boil while stirring for a further minute. Remove from heat, and cool in the refrigerator.

9 With a little melted chocolate, pipe a freehand line around the pearl shells to completely enclose them. Pour the cold sauce inside this line and then serve.

SERVES 6

A Passion
FOR
CHOCOLATE
A passion for chocolate A passion for chocolate A passion for chocolate A passion for chocolate A passion for chocolate A passion for chocolate A passion for chocolate A passion for chocolate

Chocolate Hungarian Torte

EUROPE HAS MANY FABULOUS RECIPES TO OFFER THE CHOCOLATE DEVOTEE; FEW CAN REALLY BEAT THIS MARVEL FROM HUNGARY.

5 x 60 g (2 oz) eggs, separated
⅓ cup (100 g/3½ oz) caster sugar
420 g (13 oz) dark cooking chocolate, melted
⅓ cup (90 ml/3 fl oz) milk
1¼ cups (150 g/15 oz) plain flour, sifted
200 g (6½ oz) ground almonds
¼ cup (60 g/2 oz) caster sugar, extra

DECORATION

2 tablespoons apricot jam
200 g (6½ oz) marzipan or almond paste
250 g (8 oz) dark chocolate buttons, melted (for chocolate collar)
250 g (8 oz) white chocolate buttons, melted (for collar drizzle)
250 g (8 oz) dark chocolate buttons, melted (for curls)
250 g (8 oz) white chocolate buttons, melted (for curls)

1 Preheat the oven to 150°C (300°F).

2 Grease a 20 cm (8 in) springform cake pan and line the base with baking paper.

3 Beat the egg yolks with sugar until thick and pale. Very gently fold in the chocolate by hand, then the milk, flour and almonds.

4 Beat the egg whites until very stiff and frothy and slowly blend in the extra sugar, then beat until the sugar has dissolved. Very gently fold in the chocolate mixture by hand.

5 Pour the mixture into the prepared pan and bake for 30 to 40 minutes or until the top of the cake springs back when lightly touched. Cool in the pan on a wire rack.

6 When completely cold, turn the cake out of the pan and remove the baking paper from the base. Thinly spread the top and sides of the cake with the apricot jam.

7 On a lightly floured bench, roll out the marzipan into a circle large enough to cover the top and sides of the cake. Place the marzipan over the cake and mould to fit neatly. Trim the excess marzipan.

8 *To Make Chocolate Collar.* Cut a strip of parchment paper which is long enough to wrap round the cake and 1 cm (¼ in) higher than the cake. Spread melted dark chocolate onto the paper. Wrap collar around the cake. Allow cake to stand 5 minutes in the refrigerator or until collar is firm. Remove paper from hard collar. Decorate collar with white drizzle.

9 *To Make Two-Tone Curls.* Spread white chocolate thickly on a marble slab or stainless steel bench top. Make ridges with comb. Pour melted dark chocolate over the hardened white chocolate. Pull a knife gently through the chocolate to form curls. Put the smallest curls on cake first, then largest and neatest curls, for the best effect.

10 Mark portions with a hot knife into the collar of the cake. Then cut straight through the curls to the already marked portion cuts in the collar.

SERVES 12

a Passion
FOR
CHOCOLATE

Pyramid of Dreams

One wonders, could the luxury enjoyed by the Pharaohs of Ancient Egypt really have meant anything without chocolate?

6 x 60 g (2 oz) eggs
⅔ cup (150 g/5 oz) caster sugar
1 cup (120 g/4 oz) plain flour, sifted
3 tablespoons cocoa

Chocolate Filling

1 cup (250 ml/8 fl oz) thickened cream
2½ tablespoons orange liqueur or orange juice
500 g (16 oz) white cooking chocolate, chopped
½ cup (125 ml/4 fl oz) orange liqueur, or orange juice (extra)
drinking chocolate for dusting

1 Preheat the oven to 180°C (350°F).

2 Lightly grease three 28 x 18 cm (11 x 7 in) baking pans and line each with baking paper.

3 Whisk the eggs and sugar with an electric mixer on the highest setting, or until the mixture is very thick and frothy. Lightly sprinkle the flour and cocoa over the mixture and very gently fold in by hand.

4 Pour mixture evenly between the 3 pans and using a spatula or palette knife evenly spread the mixture to the edges of each pan.

5 Bake each pan of mixture for 15 to 20 minutes or until sponge has shrunk slightly from the sides. Rest in pan for 5 minutes before turning out onto wire racks to cool.

6 *To Make Filling.* Place the cream and orange liqueur into a saucepan and bring to the boil. Remove from the heat and add the chopped white chocolate. Stir until the chocolate has melted. Pour into a dish and chill in the refrigerator, stirring occasionally, so that it does not become too thick.

7 Cut the edges off each sponge sheet along the longest edge, then cut each sheet in half again along the longest length. Sprinkle each strip with the extra orange liqueur.

8 Spread each strip thinly with the chocolate filling mixture and stack on top of each other, leaving the top strip plain. Chill the stack for 30 minutes.

9 Place the chilled cake lengthwise on the edge of a bench top. Place a ruler along the top edge of the cake furthest from you and cut diagonally through the bottom edge nearest you with a clean knife. The ruler and bench top are used to guide the knife. When cut, you will have 2 triangles of cake.

10 Stand the triangles so that the layers of cake run vertically. Join the 2 triangles together with a thin layer of the chocolate mixture to make a pyramid shape. Cover the sloping sides with the chocolate mixture and chill for 30 minutes. Dust lightly with drinking chocolate before serving.

SERVES 12

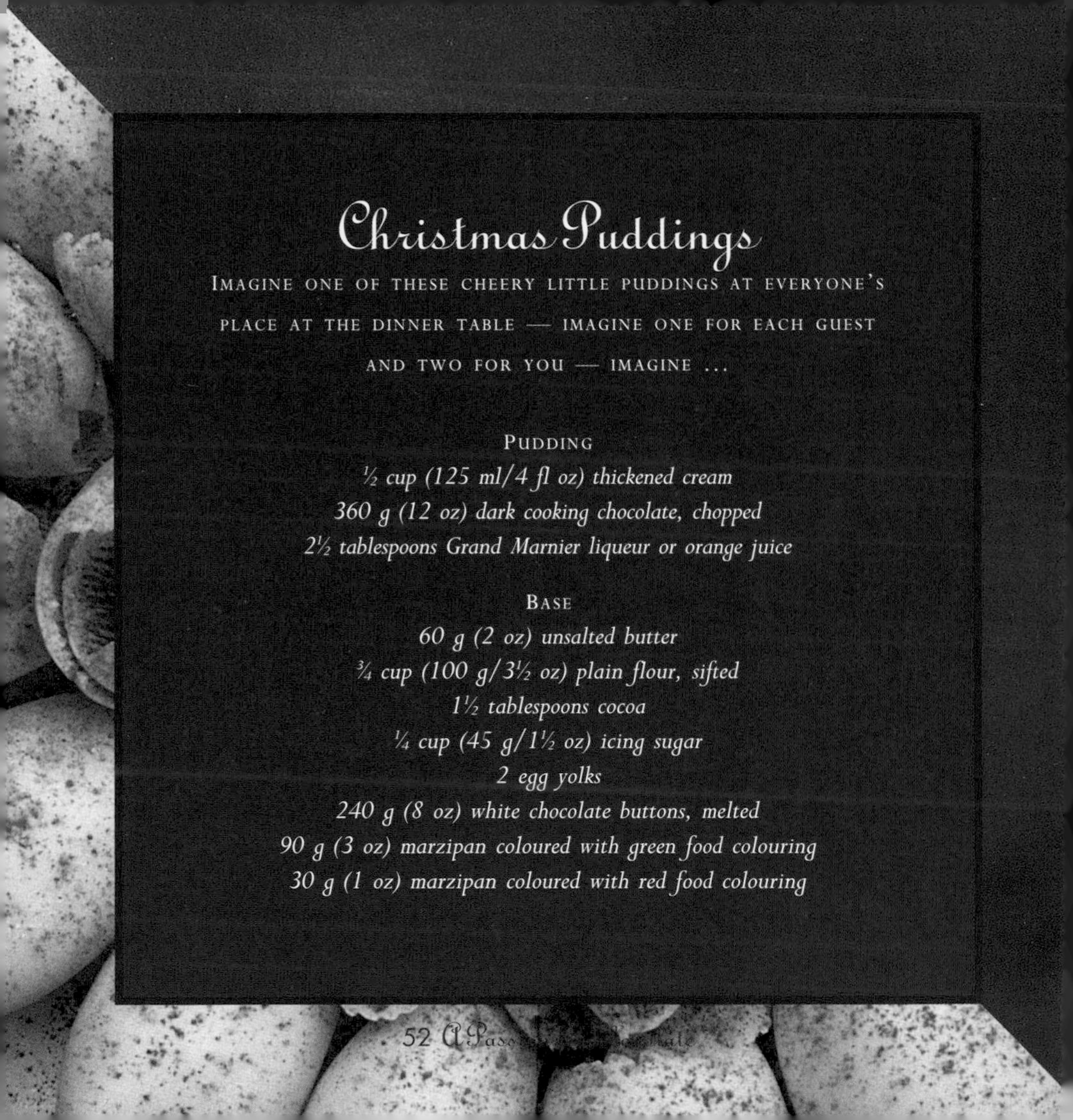

Christmas Puddings

IMAGINE ONE OF THESE CHEERY LITTLE PUDDINGS AT EVERYONE'S PLACE AT THE DINNER TABLE — IMAGINE ONE FOR EACH GUEST AND TWO FOR YOU — IMAGINE ...

PUDDING

½ cup (125 ml/4 fl oz) thickened cream
360 g (12 oz) dark cooking chocolate, chopped
2½ tablespoons Grand Marnier liqueur or orange juice

BASE

60 g (2 oz) unsalted butter
¾ cup (100 g/3½ oz) plain flour, sifted
1½ tablespoons cocoa
¼ cup (45 g/1½ oz) icing sugar
2 egg yolks
240 g (8 oz) white chocolate buttons, melted
90 g (3 oz) marzipan coloured with green food colouring
30 g (1 oz) marzipan coloured with red food colouring

1 *To Make Pudding.* Place the cream into a saucepan and bring slowly to the boil. Add the chopped chocolate and Grand Marnier and stir until the mixture becomes thick and smooth. Pour into a baking tray and refrigerate the mixture until it becomes very hard.

2 *To Make Base.* Rub butter into the flour, cocoa and icing sugar until mixture resembles fine breadcrumbs. Add egg yolk and mix thoroughly. Cover and allow the dough to rest for 5 minutes.

3 Roll the dough thinly on a lightly floured bench surface and using a 3 cm (1 in) round fluted cutter cut out approximately 14 circles.

4 Remove the chilled and solid chocolate mixture and cut it into strips. Cut the strips into 2 cm (¾ in) lengths and roll each into a ball. Place each ball onto a base circle. (If the chocolate mixture becomes a little soft to roll, place into the freezer for several minutes.)

5 Pipe a little melted white chocolate onto the top of each pudding and allow it to run slightly down the sides of the puddings.

6 Make little holly leaves by pinching little pieces of the green marzipan. Place two leaves onto the white chocolate. Roll very tiny little balls for the holly berries with the red marzipan and place three little balls per pudding on top beside the leaves.

7 Chill for 20 minutes before serving.

Makes 14

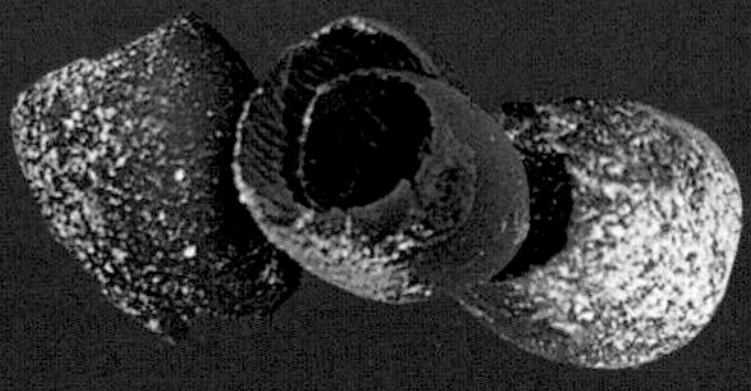

A Passion CHOCOLATE

Creative Confectionery

If your cravings for chocolate are of the twenty-four-hour type, then keep a jar of each of these sweet treats on hand so you can nibble at will. They make very desirable gifts for fellow chocoholics, too.

Dark Chocolate Fudge

A fiend for fudge? This recipe will send you to snack heaven!

2¼ cups (480 g/5½ oz) caster sugar
1¼ cups (300 ml/10 fl oz) thickened cream
120 g (4 oz) dark chocolate buttons
1 tablespoon liquid glucose
15 g (½ oz) butter

1 Combine all ingredients in a large saucepan and allow mixture to dissolve over a gentle heat. Bring mixture slowly to boil, stirring continuously and allow to boil for 6 minutes.

2 Remove saucepan from the heat and continue stirring until bubbles subside.

3 Allow mixture to cool. When cool, beat vigorously until mixture loses shine.

4 Spread into a foil-lined tray and refrigerate until set.

Makes 30 squares

White Chocolate Fudge

A smooth, light and creamy sweet treat.

2½ cups (500 g/16 oz) caster sugar
1¼ cups (300 ml/10 fl oz) thickened cream
15 g (½ oz) unsalted butter
120 g (4 oz) white chocolate buttons
1 tablespoon liquid glucose syrup
100 g (3½ oz) white chocolate buttons, extra, melted

1 Combine the sugar, cream, butter and chocolate in a large saucepan with the glucose and allow the mixture to dissolve over a gentle heat.

2 Bring the mixture slowly to the boil, stirring continuously, and boil for 7 minutes or until golden brown in colour.

3 Remove the saucepan from the heat and continue stirring until the bubbles subside. Allow the mixture to cool.

4 When cooled to lukewarm, beat vigorously until the mixture loses its shine, spread into a foil-lined tray and refrigerate until set.

5 Cut into small squares and drizzle with melted white chocolate.

Makes 24 squares

'It has been shown as proof positive that carefully prepared chocolate is as healthful a food as it is pleasant; that it is nourishing and easily digested . . . [and] that it is above all helpful to people who must do a great deal of mental work.'

BRILLAT-SAVARIN

A Passion for Chocolate

Divine Drinks & Sauces

What good would a dessert, ice cream or slice of cake be if it was served without a rich, seductive and alluring coating of chocolate sauce? And why stop at just eating chocolate? Relax and enjoy the ultimate in liquid sustenance!

Superb Chocolate Sauce

THIS DIVINELY RICH SAUCE WILL COMPLEMENT MOST DESSERTS. SERVE HOT FOR A TRULY SENSUAL EXPERIENCE.

1 cup (250 ml/8 fl oz) water
½ cup (120 g/4 oz) caster sugar
60 g (2 oz) dark cooking chocolate, chopped
¼ cup (60 ml/2 fl oz) water, extra
50 g (2 oz) cocoa, sifted
1 tablespoon cornflour, sifted
⅓ cup (90 g/3 oz) caster sugar

1 Slowly bring water, sugar and cooking chocolate to the boil in a saucepan, stirring continuously.

2 Mix the extra water with the cocoa, cornflour and caster sugar and lightly whisk to dissolve any lumps.

3 When the first mixture has boiled, slowly add the second mixture. Continually stir and allow to come to the boil again. Boil for 3 minutes and then remove from the heat.

4 Serve hot immediately or allow to cool at room temperature before storing in the refrigerator for a cold sauce.

MAKES 2½ CUPS (APPROXIMATELY)

The Ultimate Hot Chocolate

6 marshmallows
1 cup (250 ml/8 fl oz) milk, brought to the boil
1 teaspoon cocoa
1 teaspoon drinking chocolate
1 tablespoon cognac
extra cocoa for dusting

1 Place three of the marshmallows into the hot milk and stir until they have melted.

2 Pour half of the boiled milk over the cocoa and drinking chocolate and stir until they are dissolved.

3 Add the cognac to the chocolate milk and pour in the other half of the milk mixture.

4 Pour into a mug and set the other marshmallows on top of the drink and quickly dust with a little cocoa.

5 Drink while still hot.

SERVES 1 TO 2

Liqueur Sensation

A DIVINELY DECADENT SAUCE WHICH GIVES ICE CREAM A WHOLE NEW LEASE OF LIFE.

1¼ cups (300 ml/10 fl oz) water
½ cup (120 g/4 oz) caster sugar
100 g (3½ oz) dark cooking chocolate, chopped
165 g (5½ oz) milk cooking chocolate, chopped
⅓ cup (75 ml/2½ fl oz) Amaretto liqueur
1½ tablespoons (75 ml/2½ fl oz) cognac

1 Bring the water and sugar to the boil in a saucepan.

2 Add the boiled liquid to the chopped chocolate and stir until melted and the mixture is smooth.

3 Add the Amaretto and cognac to the sauce as it cools and serve immediately for the best taste.

MAKES 4 CUPS (APPROXIMATELY)

AN ANGUS & ROBERTSON PUBLICATION
Angus&Robertson, an imprint of
HarperCollins*Publishers*
25 Ryde Road, Pymble, Sydney NSW 2073, Australia
31 View Road, Glenfield, Auckland 10, New Zealand
77–85 Fulham Palace Road, London W6 8JB, United Kingdom
10 East 53rd Street, New York NY 10022, USA
First published in Australia in 1994

Design by Liz Seymour
Printed in Hong Kong

National Library of Australia
Cataloguing-in-Publication data:
Allardice, Pamela and Maree, Aaron
[Chocolate Cookery]. A passion for chocolate.
ISBN 0 207 18595 6.
1. Cookery (Chocolate). I. Title. II. Title: Chocolate cookery.
641.6374
9 8 7 6 5 4 3 2 1
97 96 95 94

passion for chocolate A passion for chocolate A passion for chocolate
A passion for chocolate A passion for chocolate A passion for chocolate
A passion for chocolate A passion for chocolate
A passion for chocolate A passion for chocolate